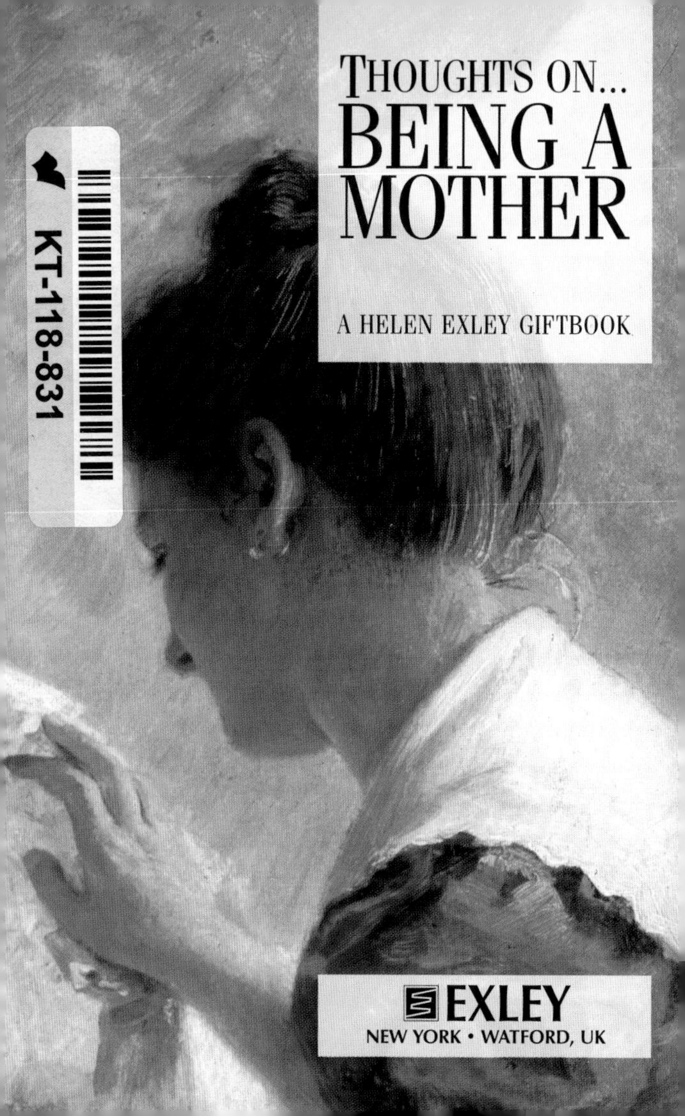

THOUGHTS ON... BEING A MOTHER

A HELEN EXLEY GIFTBOOK

EXLEY
NEW YORK • WATFORD, UK

She is yours to hold in your cupped hands, to guard and to guide. Give her your strength and wisdom and all the good that life can offer. Yours is a sacred trust.

MICHELE GUINNESS, FROM *"TAPESTRY OF VOICES"*

Life... would give her everything of consequence, life would shape her, not we. All we were good for was to make the introductions.

HELEN HAYES

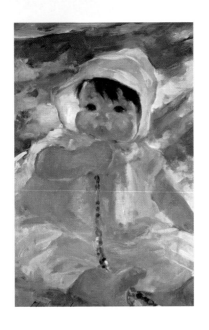

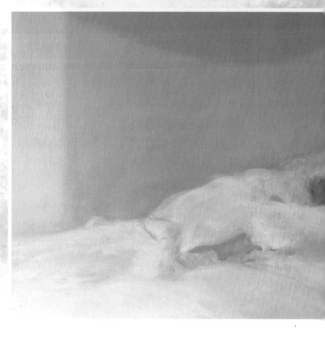

There is nothing on earth like the moment of seeing one's first baby. Men scale other heights, but there is no height like this simple one, occurring continuously throughout all the ages in musty bedrooms, in palaces, in caves and desert places. I looked at this rolled-up bundle... and knew again I had not created her. She was herself apart from me. She had her own life to lead, her

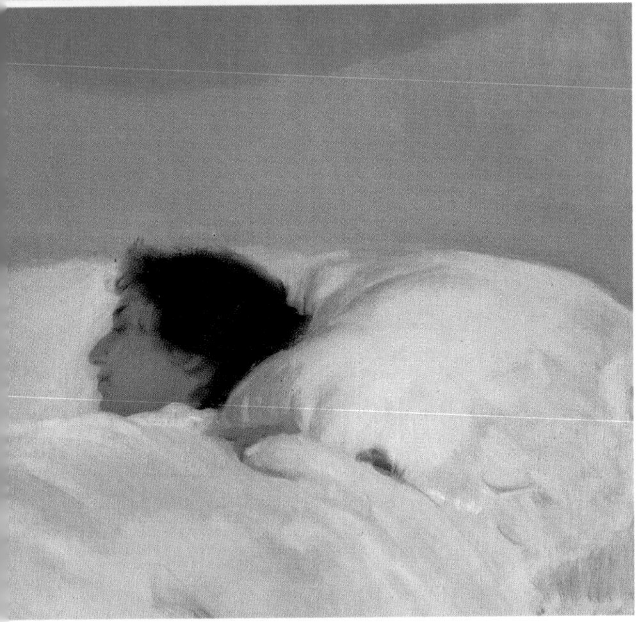

own destiny to accomplish; she just came past me to this earth. My job was to get her to adulthood and then push her off.

KATHARINE TREVELYAN, FROM *"THROUGH MINE OWN EYES"*

I think of my children's births – carry them around with me – every day of my life....

JOYCE MAYNARD

A MOTHER IS BORN

The baby was born and your life was changed
more than you ever dreamed. You found you
had sprouted invisible antennae that picked up
every alteration in breathing, every variation in
temperature, every nuance of expression in
your tiny daughter. No one told you that the
change was irreversible. That you would feel in
your own heart every pain, every loss, every
disappointment, every rebuff, every cruelty
that she experiences – life long.

ROSANNE AMBROSE-BROWN, b.1943

No one understands how someone so little can so change their world – until they hold their baby in their arms.

PAM BROWN, b.1928

GLORIOUS, MIRACULOUS BIRTH

Even ninety-year-old women still talk about childbirth. I think you tell the story over and over again to keep from feeling the loss of that experience. To have participated so directly in the creation of life and to have held that life within you is so exciting....

And every time you tell that story, you're trying to get back to the miracle.

JUDY MYERSON

Nothing is ever so important again. The washing machine may flood, the grocery bills mount up, unemployment, recession, a feud with your mother-in-law, nothing is quite the end of the world any more.... However you explain it, and however you choose to enjoy it, I guarantee you will be changed by this experience, for ever.

ESTHER RANTZEN

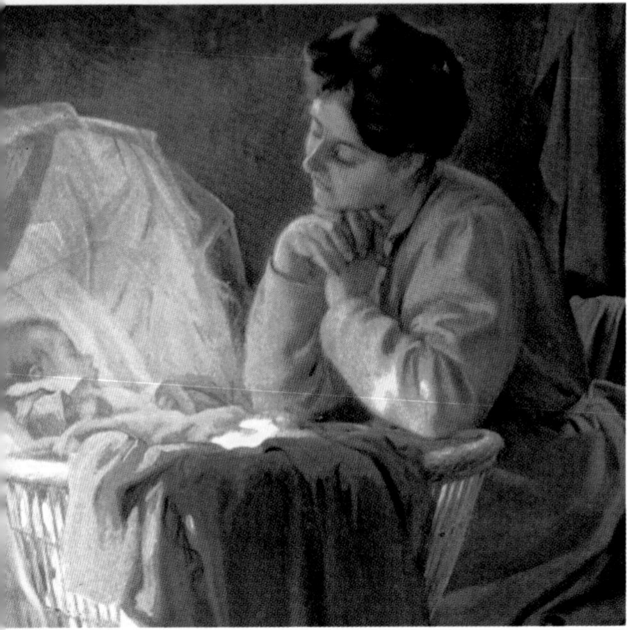

To bring a new being into this world, to see its tiny perfection and to dream of its future greatness is the most moving of all experiences and fills one with wonder and exultation.

INDIRA GANDHI (1917-1984)

YOU ARE ALL THE CHILD HAS

Every child born into this world is entitled to
its birthright
– warmth and sustenance, peace and
protection, love, laughter and the gifts
of learning
– clear waters, deep forests, stars uncountable.
The companionship of creatures.
And if any lack these things
it is the duty of every man and every woman
to make good the loss.

PAM BROWN, b.1928

Every mother who ever lived has faced that
fierce moment when a baby turns its milky
mouth to her breast and she knows she is all
it has.

ERICA JONG, b.1942, FROM "FEAR OF FIFTY"

An eternal, unconditional love

Having a child... has opened my heart in a way
that I don't believe anything else could have
done. The whole rush of feelings from a love
for your child that is so forgiving, so full.
Experiencing your own child: taking care of
that small human form, watching them reach
their milestones. There's nothing else in life like
that, although you can watch other people's
children and be part of another family. The love
for your child is an eternal, unconditional love.
Having had my own child has made me a
better person, I think. I'm more open, more
giving, more forgiving. It's probably made me
a better teacher – more compassionate and
empathetic.

DEANNE BURKE, FROM "ON WOMEN TURNING 50"

"I WANTED TO CHANGE THE WORLD..."

A mother is a woman who has taken on an extra life... she'll be two people in one skin for the rest of her days.

PAM BROWN, b.1928

[Welcoming a newborn baby was] somehow absolute, truer and more binding than any other experience life had to offer....

MARILYN FRENCH, b.1929

There is something infinitely precious about having a daughter. Mine, from the moment she was born, drew from me reserves of tenderness, protectiveness and fight I never knew I possessed. I wanted to change the world overnight, to make it a safer, easier, better place for this miniature woman, this receptacle of all my dreams and aspirations, this extension of myself.

MICHELE GUINNESS, FROM *"TAPESTRY OF VOICES"*

"EVERYTHING IS A BIT MORE…"

Your priorities change, everything changes, but the biggest change is that you love somebody in a way you have never loved before.

DIANE KEATON

Like being in love with a lover, being in love with a child colors things. You aren't to be trusted. Everything is a bit more than it seems. Everything seems a bit more than it is.

BARBARA LAZEAR ASCHER

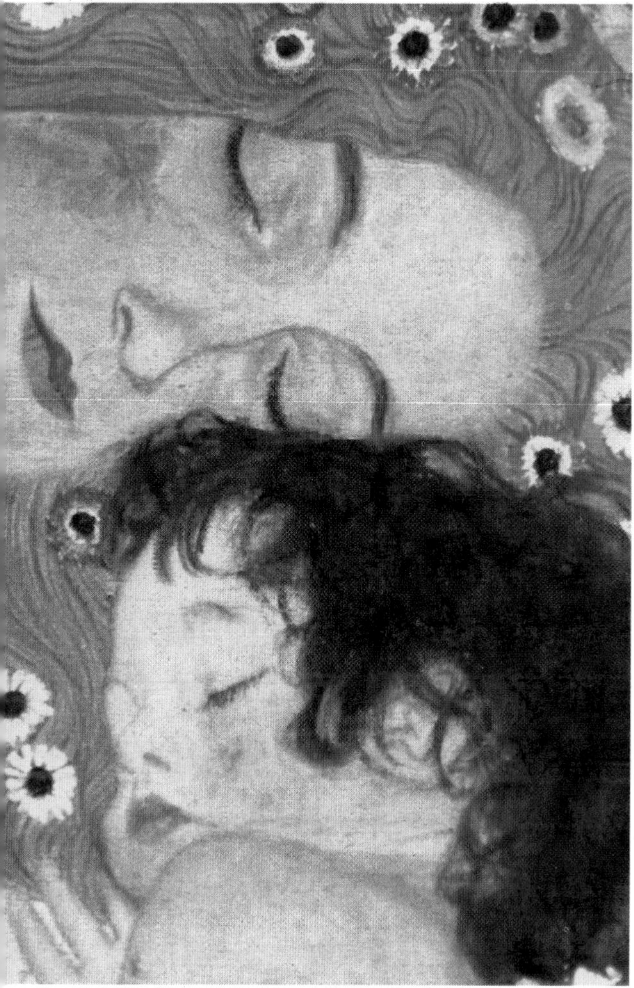

The mother's courage

In the wake of every evil inflicted by man or nature come the women, gathering what can be salvaged, the distraught and injured children, the lost, the dispossessed, the fragments of a broken society. They tear at blocks of stone tumbled by earthquake, blackened by fire. They build among the olive trees or the desert sand. Out of destruction they piece together small areas of safety.

PAM BROWN, B.1928

Mighty is the force of motherhood! It transforms all things by its vital heat; it turns timidity into fierce courage, and dreadless defiance into tremulous submission; it turns thoughtlessness into foresight, and yet stills all anxiety into calm content; it makes selfishness become self-denial, and gives even to hard vanity the glance of admiring love.

GEORGE ELIOT (MARY ANN EVANS) (1819-1880)

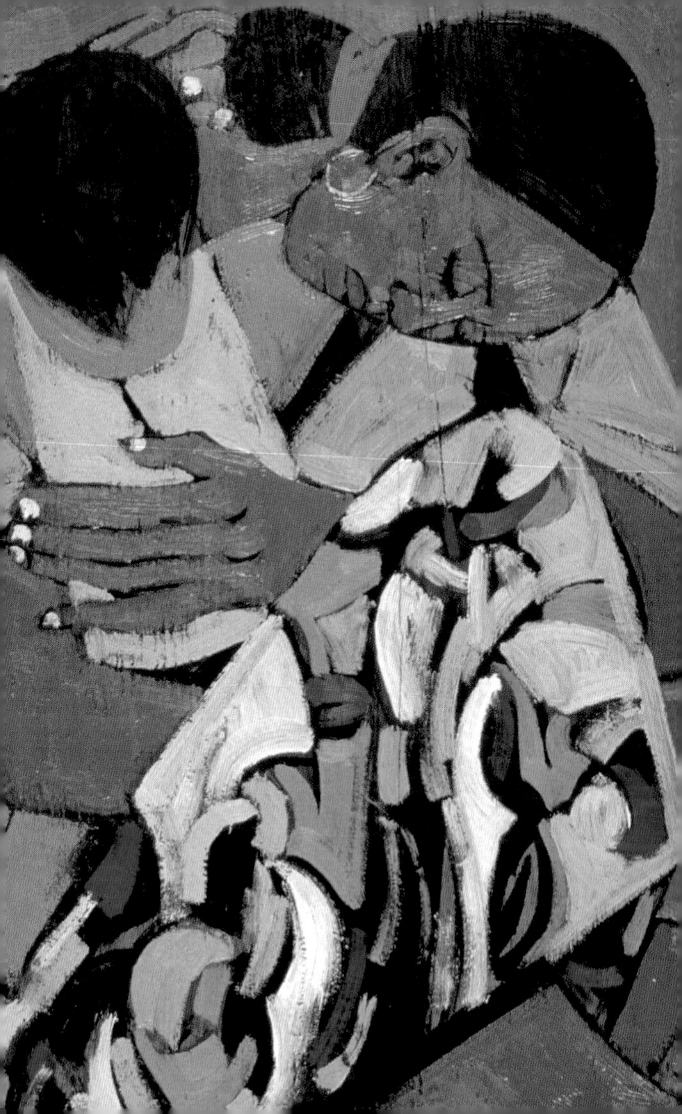

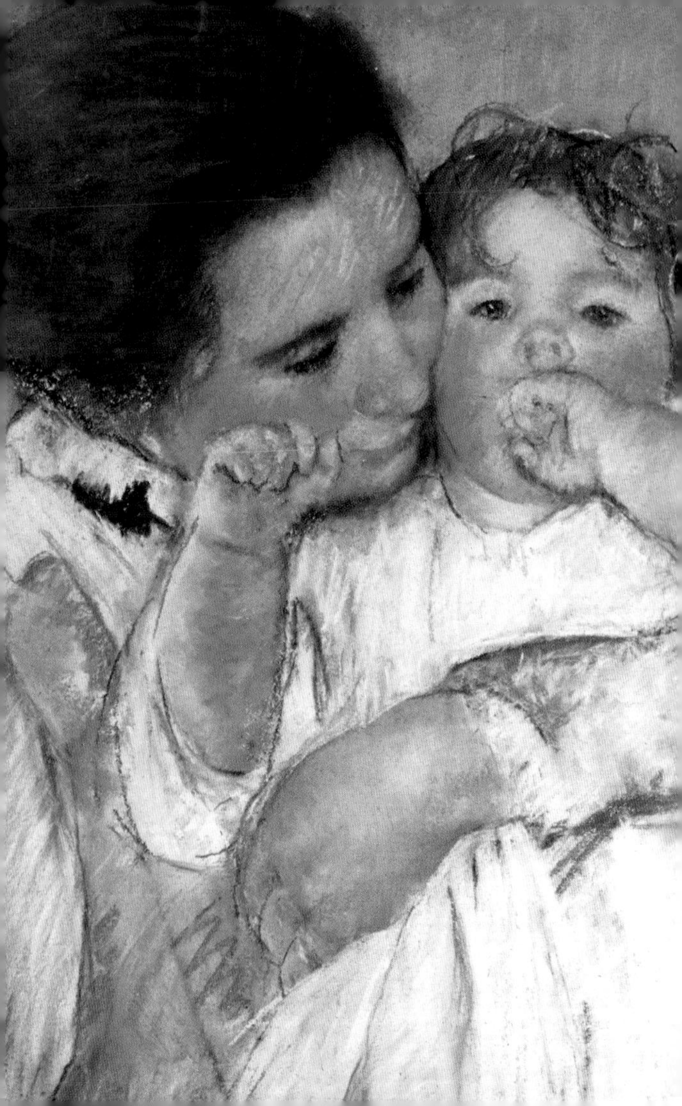

My pledge

I must teach my child the disciplines of life,
the necessary courtesies,
the little laws.
But quietly and kindly.
With love.

PAM BROWN, b.1928

I have so much I can teach her and pull out of
her. I would say you might encounter defeats
but you must never be defeated. I would teach
her to love a lot. Laugh a lot at the silliest
things and be very serious. I would teach her to
love life, I could do that.

MAYA ANGELOU, b.1928

The appealing sweetness given to the baby of the species, whether human, monkey or kangaroo, is nature's guileful way of enslaving the mother. Most mothers... although remaining aware of "the sentence of motherhood", manage to concentrate on the rewards. These range from the sheer fun of a gurgling, rolling, squeaking plaything in the home, to the passionate intensity of the love which many mothers feel for their babies. Often this will surpass their feelings for their husband or any man....

RACHEL BILLINGTON, FROM *"THE GREAT UMBILICAL"*

"Don't negotiate with terrorists," cautions her father when she yodels to be picked up. Absolutely right of course. But when he's left the room, I find myself moving towards her, drawn by that irresistible beat.

ALLISON PEARSON

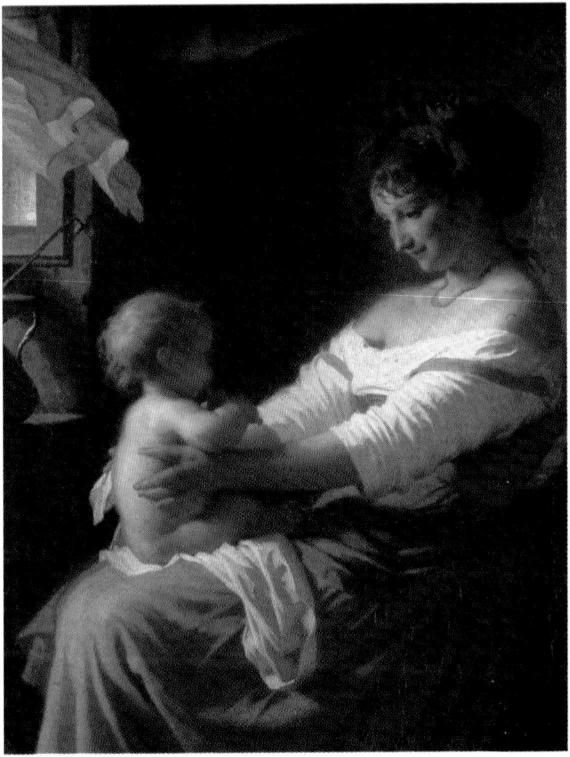

A RECOGNITION OF LOVE

She looked up at me. Recognition, a memory of
two souls. She relaxed. The crying stopped.
Her eyes melted through me, forging a
connection in me with their soft heat. I felt her
love power stir in my heart.

SHIRLEY MACLAINE, b.1934, FROM *"DANCE WHILE YOU CAN"*

Gradually I began to realize that she liked me, that she had no option to liking me, and that unless I took great pains to alienate her she would go on liking me, for a couple of years at least. It was very pleasant to receive such uncritical love, because it left me free to bestow love; my kisses were met by small warm rubbery unrejecting cheeks and soft dovey mumblings of delight.

MARGARET DRABBLE, b.1939, FROM *"THE MILLSTONE"*

... I had discovered true love. The love which repays slavery and exhaustion with a brief smile. But what a smile! It was more than enough. My present prostration was somehow sweeter than all the pleasures of my past life.

SUE LIMB, FROM *"LOVE FORTY"*

GROWING TO LOVE BEING ORDINARY

Its [motherhood's] demands are so compelling, so clearly important, and also so profoundly satisfying.
... You give up your self, and finally you don't even mind. You become your child's guide to life at the expense of that swollen ego you thought so immutable. I wouldn't have missed this for anything. It humbled my ego and stretched my soul. It awakened me to eternity. It made me know my own humanity, my own mortality, my own limits. It gave me whatever crumbs of wisdom I possess today.

ERICA JONG, b.1942, FROM *"FEAR OF FIFTY"*

The greatest gift that my kids give me is the reminder that I'm not so great. I'm just ordinary.

DIANA ROSS

Motherhood is an acquired taste. You learn it
humbled on your knees.

ERICA JONG, b.1942, FROM "FEAR OF FIFTY"

It is not until you become a mother that your judgement slowly turns to compassion and understanding.

ERMA BOMBECK, b.1927

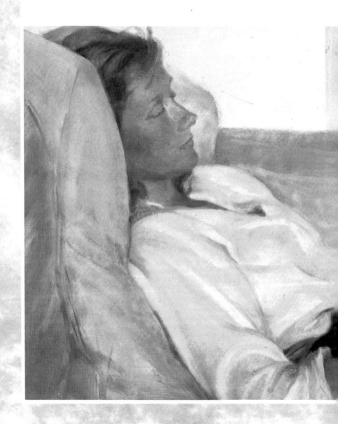

We women have always been the ones to construct and piece together sanctuary and refuge for all our people – our neighborhoods, our family.

JUNE JORDAN

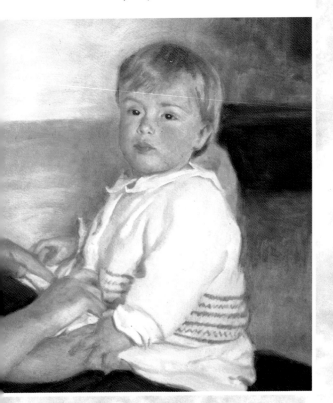

Hassle, hassle and hard work

One hour with a child is like a ten-mile run.

JOAN BENOIT SAMUELSON,
FROM *"NEW YORK TIMES"*, 1991

I think there should be a compound where they send people who want to be parents. They should have to spend a week there, being pelted with vomit and poo, and being woken up once an hour every night.

KATHY LETTE

There is no such thing as a NON-working mother.

HESTER MUNDIS

Nothing else ever will make you as happy or as sad, as proud or as tired, for nothing is quite as hard as helping a person develop his own individuality especially while you struggle to keep your own.

MARGUERITE KELLY AND ELIA PARSONS

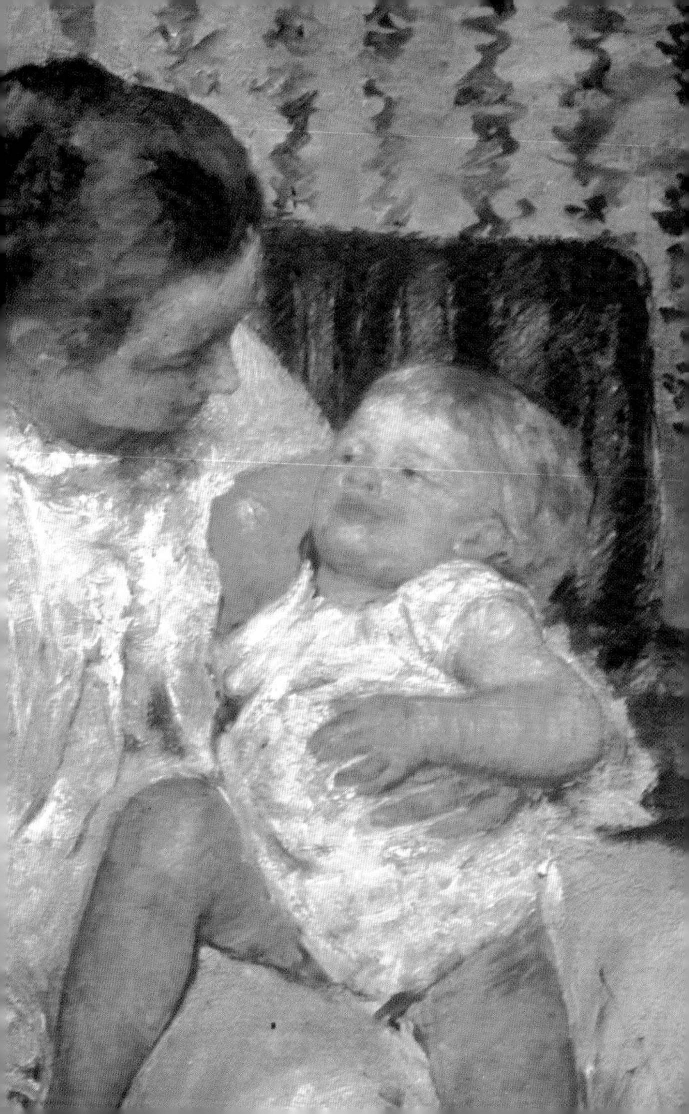

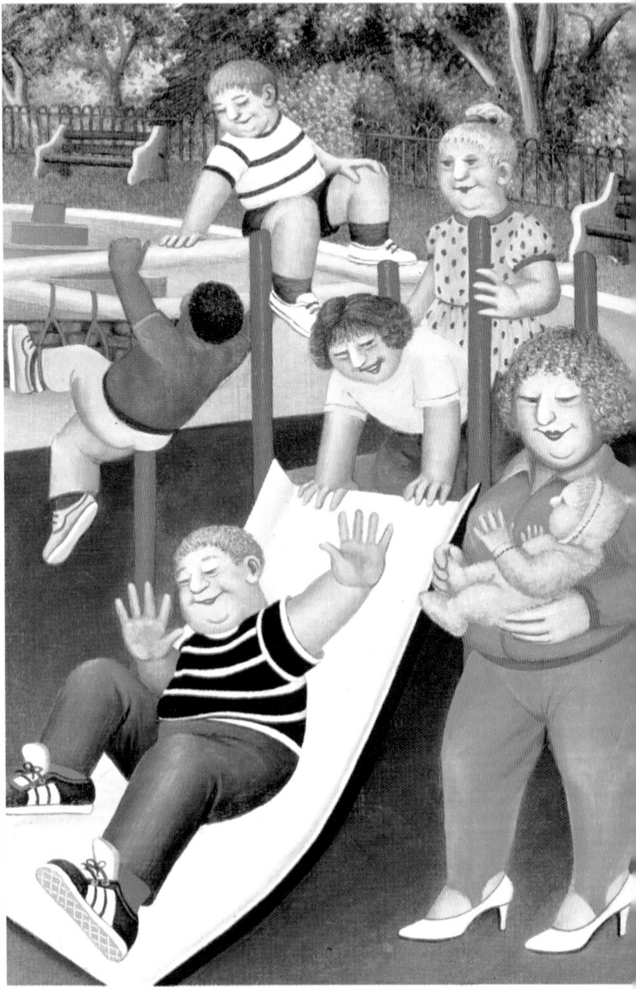

A HAZARD COURSE!

Every mother hopes and believes she won't
make the mistakes she made with the first child
second time round.
She doesn't.
She makes an entirely different lot.

PAM BROWN, b.1928

Before embarking on any task, however trivial,
a mother mentally runs it through – looking for
the opportunities for self-destruction that any
child will spot... and seize upon.

CHARLOTTE GRAY

Adorable children are considered to be the
general property of the human race. (Rude
children belong to their mothers.)

**JUDITH MARTIN, FROM *"MISS MANNERS' GUIDE TO REARING
PERFECT CHILDREN"***

Mothers sometimes feel like wearing a placard
– "Everyone's buck stops here."

PAM BROWN, b.1928

A MOTHER IS A PERSON

a mother is a person
who gives birth
cleans up messes
kisses dirty faces
makes thousands of peanut butter sandwiches
and says no more often than yes

a mother is a person
who acts as chauffeur
personal secretary
and general contractor
housebreaks and feeds the dog
hunts for numerous articles
and hurts when her child is hurt

a mother is a person
who needs to remember
she is a person

MARY ELEANORE RICE,
FROM "IMAGES: WOMEN IN TRANSITION"

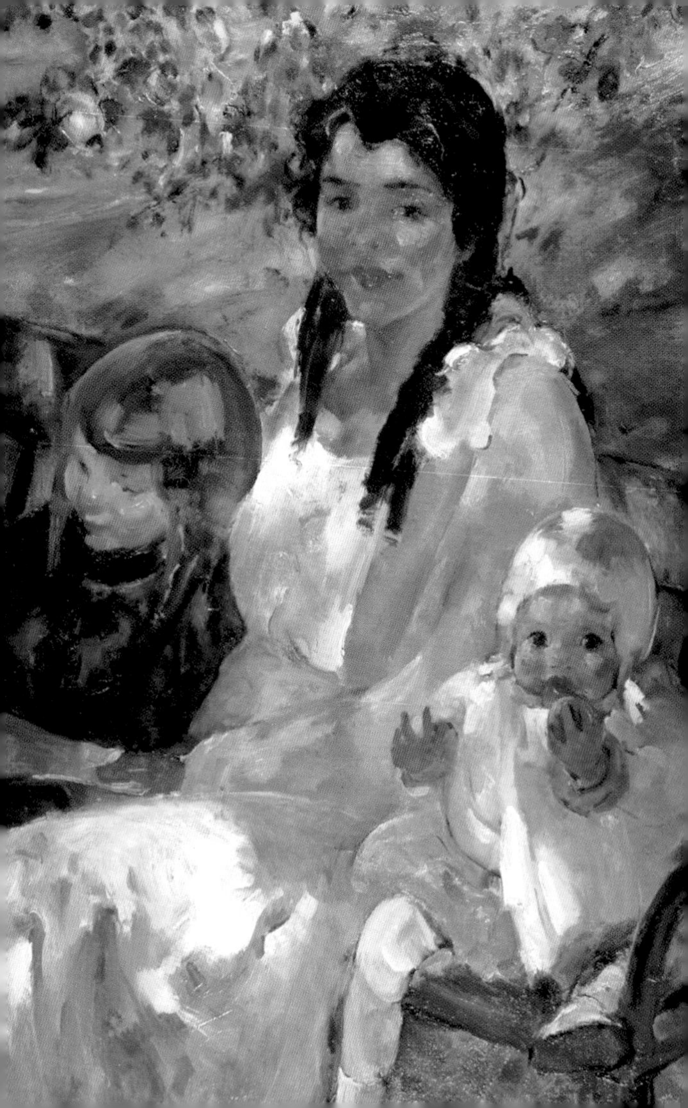

It will all be over so quickly

It will be gone before you know it. The fingerprints on the wall appear higher and higher. Then suddenly they disappear.

DOROTHY EVSLIN

Whoever said it first spoke with insight and wisdom: you don't own children, you only borrow them.

ANNE LINN

Little things outlast great triumphs. Here is the ghost of little fingers clasping your hand, here are arms stretched out to greet you; here is a face uplifted for your kiss. The child has grown and gone away – and yet the sweetness stays.

PAM BROWN, b.1928

The importance of a mother

A child's hand in yours – what tenderness it arouses, what power it conjures. You are instantly the very touchstone of wisdom and strength.

MARJORIE HOLMES,
FROM "CALENDAR OF LOVE AND INSPIRATION"

No kiss given to a child is ever lost, no showing of delight, no touch of reassurance, no song, no tale of wonder. They will be part of all that it becomes.

PAM BROWN, b.1928

I believe that motherhood is the greatest role of my life. Nothing, not even winning an Oscar, can compete with the pleasure and sense of accomplishment it has given me.

SOPHIA LOREN, b.1934

Judicious mothers will always keep in mind that they are the first book read, and the last put aside in every child's library.

C. LENNOX REDMOND

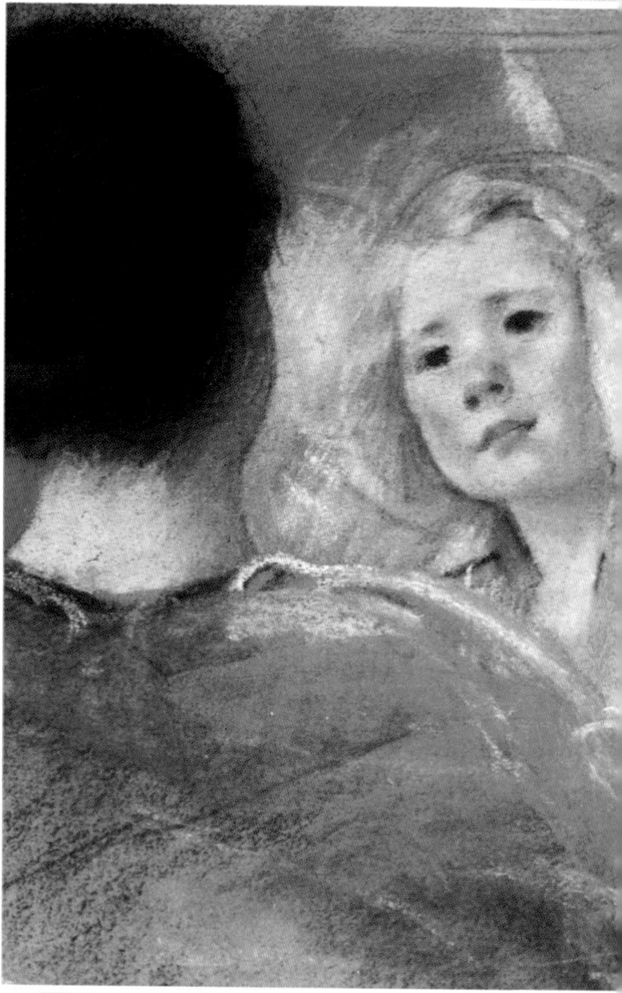

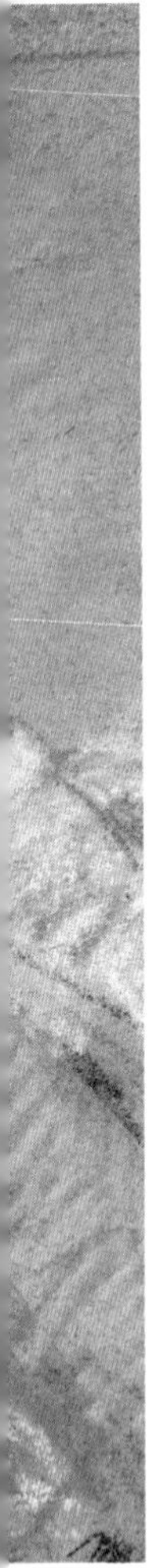

Through a child's eyes we rediscover the world's loveliness and mystery.

PAM BROWN, b.1928

Instead of the blank wall I had feared, a new landscape was opening up. My daughter was leading me, paradoxically, around to the very beginning of things: backwards through the looking glass into a wonderland where dusty old memories stirred, unfurled themselves and gleamed gold-vermilion.

SUE LIMB, FROM *"LOVE FORTY"*

A DREAM FOR MY CHILDREN

My dream for Ashley and Alexandra is to raise
them to be all they can be, to nurture them into
responsible, loving, secure, giving, human
beings who not only find, but aren't afraid to
go after, whatever it is that makes them happy
in life.

VANESSA BELL CALLOWAY

I think that by showing my children as many
facets of life as possible they will be able to
make their own choice. I do not want to
prevent them from learning about anything. All
I wish to do is give them the encouragement to
be themselves, and turn them on to all the
things in life which are beautiful and
worthwhile.

CAROLINE COOK

Dealing with little monsters

Kids never believe their mother has something she'd rather be doing than washing their jeans.

CHARLOTTE GRAY

Parenthood; that state of being better chaperoned than you were before marriage.

MARCELENE COX

Mothers are people who stay up till midnight to get a shepherd's dress made from a bath towel by morning. Because the shepherd had forgotten to mention the Nativity Play till the night before. Thanks, Mum.

PAM BROWN, b.1928

A mother is neither cocky, nor proud, because she knows the school principal may call at any minute to report that her child had just driven a motorcycle through the gymnasium.

MARY KAY BLAKELY

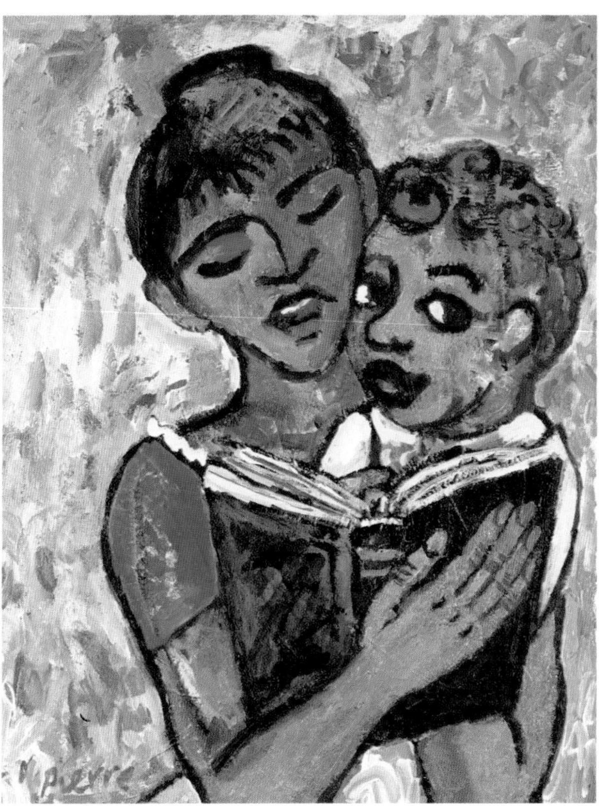

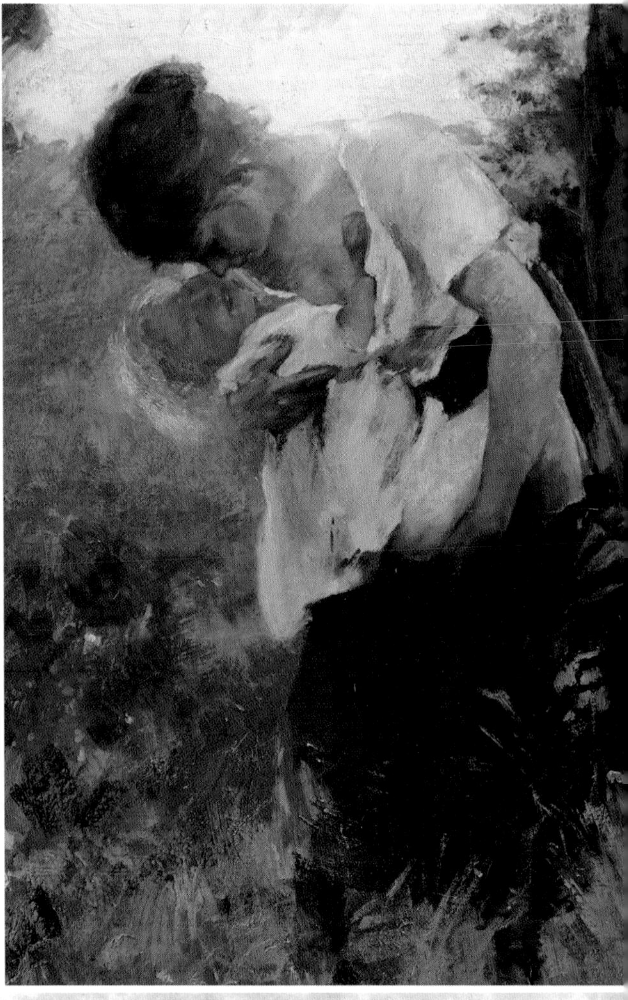

PURE HAPPINESS!

A mother has the best excuse yet to paddle in fountains, dig canals in the sand, climb trees, shriek on fairground rides, wallow in ponds, swoosh down slides, read aloud all the stories she loves best, declaim poems, act Lady Macbeth, dance the Dying Swan, sing the blues, roly-poly down hillsides, make mud pies, explore museums and run egg and spoon races.

PAM BROWN, b.1928

My idea of heaven is having time with [my children].

MICHELLE PFEIFFER

I say to people that having children is the best thing that's ever happened to me, and I utterly believe it. It's even better than marriage – it's like an extension of marriage. Just to look at your children, and to think you actually created them with your husband, is the most extraordinary feeling, and then to see bits of yourself emerge in them, and bits of him too, and to argue with them and realize that they're individuals, they are part of you and yet are absolutely separate – it's extraordinary.

ANNA CARTARET, FROM *"WOMEN"*

To me motherhood has been the most beautiful thing in my life. The wonder of it never ceases for me – to see you all developing from tiny helpless babies into big strong girls and boys, to see your minds changing with your years and to remember that some day you will be grown men and women. It is overwhelming.

MRS COLBERT, IN A LETTER TO HER DAUGHTER JANE

Living your own life

The woman is greater than the wife and
mother, and in consenting to take upon herself
these relationships she should never sacrifice
one iota of her individuality.

ELIZABETH CADY STANTON (1815-1902)

Above the titles of wife and mother, which, although dear, are transitory and accidental, there is the title human being, which precedes and outranks every other.

MARY ASHTON LIVERMORE (1820-1905)

Mothers should perform a small exercise night and morning. They should repeat, very firmly, their own names. The name that they had before they were wives or mothers. The name of the skilled, independent woman with a multitude of interests that they once were. And are. And are. And are.

PAM BROWN, b.1928

The most important legacy a mother can leave her children is the quality of her own life.

JOAN HULL

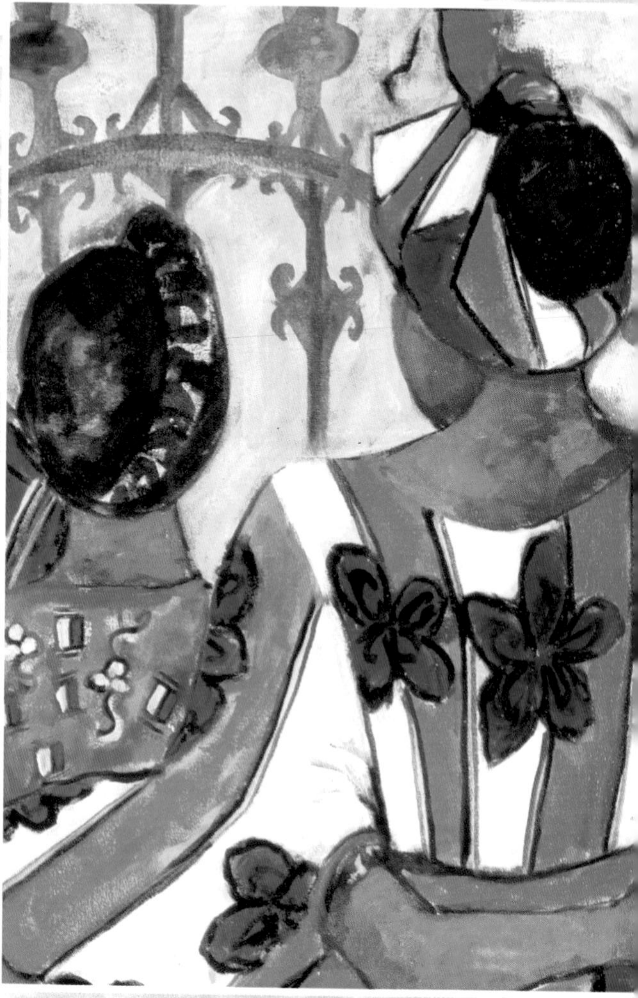

Your children are always your "babies", even if they have grey hair.

JANET LEIGH, b.1927

... the mother whose heart has been plucked out to make a sacrifice on the altar of poetry or fiction or love or freedom still says, when the grown child stumbles, "Are you hurt, my child?"

ERICA JONG, b.1942, FROM "FEAR OF FIFTY"

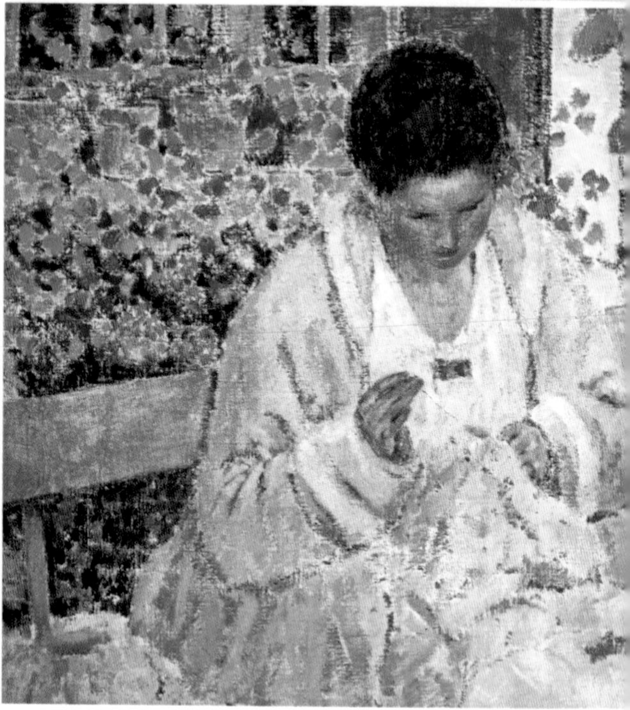

Human creatures go about their lives, busy and concerned – and scarcely notice the figure in the window, in the corner, in the shadows. A mother watches forever – and space and time are nothing to her.

PAM BROWN, b.1928

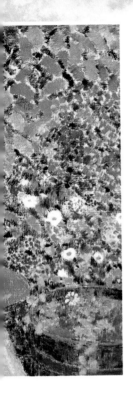

In spite of the accumulation of signals flagging the onset of adulthood, nothing really prepares you for the wrenching moment when your child, who towers over you and has a black belt in karate, is no longer yours. From the first tiny, eerie drumming of the foetal heartbeat, you have an intimation of independence, a subcutaneous sense that this minute life is getting along fine on its own.

ANNE LINN

The pain of letting go

There are only two lasting bequests we can hope to give our children. One is roots; the other, wings.

AUTHOR UNKNOWN

You spend close on a couple of decades preparing your child to leave you; you succeed; the reward is pain and silence.

ANNE LINN

The everlasting sadness of any mother is that there comes a time when she can no longer bring magic to your life, nor cure your troubles.

DIANA BRISCOE

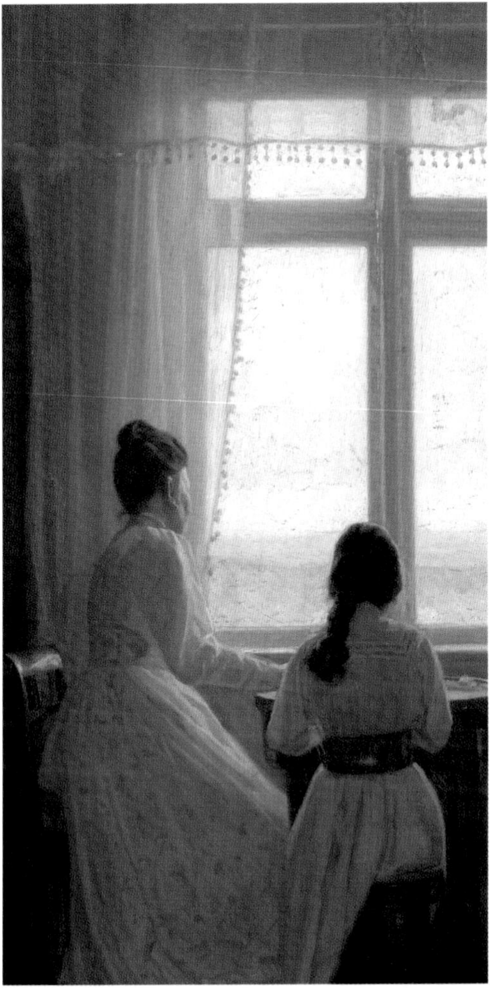